CHARGING THE
YEAR 2000

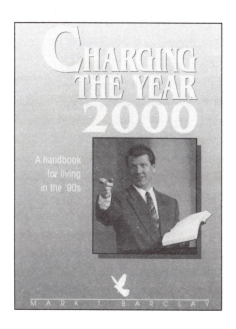

Copyright 1991
A
MARK T. BARCLAY
PUBLICATION
All Rights Reserved

Printed in the United States of America

ISBN 0-944802-13-3

Cover Design
Heart Art & Design
501 George Street
Midland, MI 48640

CHARGING THE YEAR 2000

Table of Contents

CHAPTER 1
SIGNS OF THE TIMES

"And Jesus went out, and departed from the temple: and his disciples came to him for to shew him the buildings of the temple.

And Jesus said unto them, See ye not all these things? verily I say unto you, There shall not be left here one stone upon another, that shall not be thrown down.

And as he sat upon the mount of Olives, the disciples came unto him privately, saying, Tell us, when shall these things be? and what shall be the sign of thy coming, and of the end of the world?"

Matthew 24:1-3

This is still the question that is asked most often today, and may very well be the question of the decade. For those people who are not familiar with the contents of the Bible, questions like these are even more fearful and add to the confusion of an unsaved, unrenewed mind. The Bible is the only thing on the earth that interprets the times for us. It is significantly clear about the outcome of people, as well as the earth itself.

1

"And Jesus answered and said unto them, Take heed that no man deceive you.

For many shall come in my name, saying, I am Christ; and shall deceive many.

And ye shall hear of wars and rumours of wars: see that ye be not troubled: for all these things must come to pass, but the end is not yet.

For nation shall rise against nation, and kingdom against kingdom: and there shall be famines, and pestilences, and earthquakes, in divers places.

All these are the beginning of sorrows."

Matthew 24:4-8

Here are the answers that Jesus gave to these awesome questions. They are still good for today. I'll list the predictions of Jesus Christ.

JESUS WARNS OF DECEIVERS

Jesus said, ". . . take heed that no man deceive you." We were warned almost two thousand years ago that there would be men who would deceive us if we did not take heed. Jesus also warned us how these deceivers would come to us. He said, "For many shall come in my name, saying, I am the Christ; and shall deceive many."

Can you imagine people coming to us in Jesus' name? Man, this is the password of all passwords. Almost all

2

Christians are prone to be soft and sensitive towards anyone who uses this famous name. It is a name that is commonly known for its majesty, royalty, and authority. Most Christians are so naive that they believe anyone who presents that name.

If we take heed, just like Jesus said, then we will not be one of those who is led astray. Check out the following verse.

> *"Then if any man shall say unto you, Lo, here is Christ, or there; believe it not.*
>
> *For there shall arise false Christs, and false prophets, and shall shew great signs and wonders; insomuch that, if it were possible, they shall deceive the very elect."*
>
> Matthew 24:23-24

Even the very elect shall be deceived—if it were possible. This is pretty heavy deception for the elect to be in danger of it. I suppose that the very elect cannot be deceived by these false ministers and signs and wonders. Jesus taught that a perverse generation seeks signs. For the believers, signs and wonders follow the preaching of the Word and them that believe.

My faith says that no elect person can be deceived to the degree of falling away. However, I must admit that lately I have seen enough people who were off course to begin to take note. Besides, why would Jesus warn his men about these things if there was no danger involved for them?

MANY DECEIVE MANY,
SOME TRULY LEAD SOME

Notice in verse five (quoted before) that Jesus warns us of **many** coming in his name to deceive. How many? Many! How many? Many! If you compare this to the book of Ephesians, chapter four, you'll see that there are only **some** true ministers—**some** apostles, prophets, evangelists, pastors, and teachers—only some, but **many** false ones.

> *"And many false prophets shall rise, and shall deceive many."*
>
> Matthew 24:11

Jesus also added to this by teaching us about the two gates at the end of this life. There was a narrow gate with a straight road to it, and there was a wide gate that was easily found. This story told by Christ tells us that **many** there be that enter into the wide gate but only **few** that even find the narrow one. **Many** false ministers and people will deceive **many** to include, perhaps, some of the very elect . . . if it is possible. Only **some** truly appointed ministers will help **some** (few) find the right way. How sad!

> *"Enter ye in at the strait gate: for wide is the gate, and broad is the way, that leadeth to destruction, and many there be which go in thereat:*
>
> *Because strait is the gate, and narrow is the way, which leadeth unto life, and few there be that find it."*
>
> Matthew 7:13-14

4

If you are a minister, I pray that you are one of those that Jesus set in the church. If you are a believer, I pray you are one of those who will find the straight road leading to the narrow gate of eternal life.

The Bible warns us that even false ministers will do great signs and wonders. In the last days you will not be able to decipher false from true by outward performances or manifestations (study Matthew 24:24).

In Matthew 7:22 Jesus tells us of a certain people who will look very anointed—but would not be of Christ. They would twice say, "Lord." They would prophesy, cast out devils, do many wonderful works, and know how to use the name of Jesus. In fact, they would do all these things in that name. Yet, Jesus declared that he had never known them and demanded that they depart from him. Watch out for these. Remember, you cannot tell if someone is of Christ or not by their outward manifestations. (See our book *Preachers of Righteousness*.)

JESUS PREDICTS A DAY OF SLANDER

"And ye shall hear of wars and rumours of wars: see that ye be not troubled: for all these things must come to pass, but the end is not yet.

For nation shall rise against nation, and kingdom against kingdom . . ."

Matthew 24:6-7

Without taking these things out of context, we apply the word "nations" as "people." It could, of course, apply to the countries of the world as well. For many years I have heard

5

people talk about the wars that are going on worldwide, and as they monitor them, they say it is a sign of the times. But you know, there have always been conflicts and wars and battles between nations far before anyone was in the last of the last days.

I want to alert you to something here that could actually save you many crises. Notice that Jesus predicts the misuse of mouths as the real problem to watch out for. He said, ". . . ye shall hear of . . . and . . . rumors of . . . " There seems to be just as large an emphasis on rumors and hearsay as there is on actual wars. This is certainly descriptive of the day in which we live.

It is very difficult today to do anything in the ministry— or for Jesus—without somebody speaking against it. This is the day of gossip. Talebearing and dissension are the everyday part of many Christians' lives. It is very difficult to even find ministers to sup with that don't spend all their time putting down another.

We live in a decade where people have no fear to openly gossip or slander each other or the ministry gifts. It will get worse as the day approaches and the decade comes to a close. Even now, and it will continue, some unruly teachers even slander other ministers right from the pulpit. They call it exposing sin and revealing the heresy, but it mostly just amounts to slander.

There is now, and there will continue to be, even more name-calling in public assemblies. Some will interpret this as right, but most of it will be a shame to them and a disgrace to the work of the gospel. Many will major in minors and walk right off course through their own infatuations. Many will take someone else's word for it and won't study for themselves, so they will walk as workmen who are consistently ashamed.

The wise ministers and believers will study for themselves, like the Bereans of the Bible, and they will be extra cautious with their mouths.

> *". . . see that ye be not troubled: for all these things must come to pass . . ."*
> Matthew 24:6

JESUS PREDICTED A COMPETITIVE SPIRIT

Our Lord Jesus predicted that some individual ministers, as well as groups of them, would claim to have the anointing and the word of the hour. Not all of these competitive preachers and teachers will be false. Even some true ones will get caught up in this shameful scramble for preeminence.

They will cry out that they are the anointed ones. "Come over to us," they will say, "We have the word of the hour, and God is using us and us alone." We see this again in Matthew 24:24. They were crying out that they were the Christ (the anointed one or ones) to draw disciples to themselves.

Don't get caught up with those who claim themselves to be great leaders or to have important anointings. Beware especially of those who always put others down. Beware of those who isolate themselves from the rest of the Body. Beware of individual ministers, believers, churches, and ministerial groups that politic and woo you to uproot your base and join them.

JESUS PREDICTED LAWLESSNESS

"And because iniquity shall abound, the love of many shall wax cold.

But he that shall endure unto the end, the same shall be saved."

Matthew 24:12-13

Jesus also predicted misbehavior among men and hardening of hearts in the last days. He told us of lawlessness increasing and people being affected by it. Lawlessness, basically, is living and acting according to one's heart of iniquity instead of the scriptures. When anyone does this, they almost always affect others—negatively. When people struggle through church splits, family splits, and say things against their loved ones and pastors, they get hurt and sometimes bitter.

When this hurt or bitterness rests in them, it causes them to lose their fervency for serving Jesus. This, of course, causes people to go from red-hot to really cold. This is exactly what Jesus was talking about when he referred to some growing cold. One version of this verse tells us that the love of **most** will grow cold. This is not only a shame, but a scary thought.

To have grown cold is a treacherous condition to be in. In order to grow cold, you must have been hot at one time. In growing cold, you must pass through the lukewarm stage—which could get you spewn out of His mouth. A cool heart will paralyze you.

Pray for all Christians everywhere that they will not be affected by this lawless living or by others who practice it. Pray that they will stay hot and not grow cold. When your love grows cold, all things cool off because love is your propulsion.

This is all quite a shame. Today is the day that the Lord needs us the most.

CHAPTER 2
THE END OF THE AGE

"Blow ye the trumpet in Zion, and sound an alarm in my holy mountain: let all the inhabitants of the land tremble: for the day of the LORD cometh, for it is nigh at hand;

A day of darkness and of gloominess, a day of clouds and of thick darkness . . ."

Joel 2:1-2

"For, behold, the darkness shall cover the earth, and gross darkness the people: but the LORD shall arise upon thee, and his glory shall be seen upon thee."

Isaiah 60:2

"And ye shall hear of wars and rumours of wars: see that ye be not troubled: for all these things must come to pass, but the end is not yet.

All these are the beginning of sorrows."

Matthew 24:6, 8

The scripture references on this subject are too numerous, in both the Old and New Testaments, to quote here. There are very consistent references that show us the end of the age will be filled with drastically opposing forces. The world will by all means grow worse, but the church will be triumphant and prevail. I would much rather face the glory than the gross darkness.

This very easily could be the last decade. No man knows for sure, but many feel it is. Almost all the Bible scholars are referring to this decade as perhaps the last. The Lord Jesus could very easily come within the next few years.

We are, at the time of this writing, just nine years from the greatest millennial change ever to face mankind. The Year 2000 is about to come upon us. Can you even imagine what it will be like if the Lord doesn't come? Can you even imagine what we will invent and what the height of our technology will be?

In the eighties, men started wearing earrings, women didn't want to be called female, and teens spiked and painted their hair. In the eighties, the only sin was not to win. Success was the top of the corporate ladder, and there seemed to be nothing too low, practiced by man, to get him there. The eighties released rapists and murderers from their sentences and jailed preachers for excessive terms. We are paying the price now for the wages of their sin in our society. What a decade it was.

The nineties will bring judgment upon society, and it will retch from the very fear of it. Even the most important of all will face fear of failure, and kings will turn against presidents. They will submit themselves to frustration—and still not find the total solution for peace and prosperity. Man will, like never before, waste—and even destroy—his life-sustaining elements.

JESUS PREDICTED UNUSUAL HAPPENINGS

"For nation shall rise against nation, and kingdom against kingdom: and there shall be famines, and pestilences, and earthquakes, in divers places."

Matthew 24:7

"For then shall be great tribulation, such as was not since the beginning of the world to this time, no, nor ever shall be.

And except those days should be shortened, there should no flesh be saved: but for the elect's sake those days shall be shortened."

Matthew 24:21-22

"Immediately after the tribulation of those days shall the sun be darkened, and the moon shall not give her light, and the stars shall fall from heaven, and the powers of the heavens shall be shaken."

Matthew 24:29

Already we hear of unusual happenings in the world—just as Jesus predicted. We have record frosts in the South wiping out crops, while the North fights off rapid thaws causing great flooding.

CHARGING THE YEAR 2000

The damage done by hurricanes, tornadoes, typhoons, ice storms, lightning strikes, heavy winds, hail, and record rainfall is outrageous.

Almost no country of the world escapes the death-striking blow of famine. Even here in the United States where there is surplus, we have people suffering because they cannot get proper supply for their families. One of the greatest preachers of our day presented study findings that indicate more people died of hunger in a given year than all the casualties of both world wars. Wow!

Earthquakes have become an almost regular part of evening news. Cities even gather now in advance waiting for such predictions to come to pass. The death toll is high, and the damage is into the multiple millions.

Does it sound doomsdayish? Well, Jesus is the one who first proclaimed it as part of the end times.

Sometimes I wonder if these great men of God mentioned in the Bible, when they had their visions, really did see the sky filled with our satellites, space stations, and shuttles? I wonder if John the Revelator really did see star wars?

JESUS PREDICTED GREAT FEAR AMONG MEN

"Men's hearts failing them for fear, and for looking after those things which are coming on the earth: for the powers of heaven shall be shaken."

Luke 21:26

12

It would be silly to say that all the heart attacks and heart failures of the day are due to this fear. However, I can promise you that some of them are. In the days to come, men will be greater worriers, and they will fret themselves to death. Stress will become an antagonizing companion to those who don't walk by faith. This stress, already known by man as a killer, will haunt the human race—stripping it of even the physically strong and young.

To have warning is to take warning. It always helps to know what is coming next. That way you can prepare for it and fortify yourself. I know that many Christians will be just like the world and will suffer loss, but others will take strength in God and endure until the end.

Those who walk in the Spirit will be fine. Terrorism, plane crashes, explosions, crime, and horror will not overcome them. As they overcome the fear of these things, they will be overcomers themselves. Even the diseases of the day will not devastate the body of Christ. When they use the Word of God to win the battle in their minds, then they will win the battle.

JESUS PREDICTED
SUPERNATURAL MANIFESTATION

". . . false Christs, and false prophets, and shall shew great signs and wonders; insomuch that, if it were possible, they shall deceive the very elect."

Matthew 24:24

There are many scriptures that could be inserted here. The fact that the end is near will cause Satan to launch his best deceptive measures and his greatest display of power—all to be trampled upon by the powers of God, I might add.

The satanic church is coming out of hiding and is almost now in full display. The churches that permit manifestations of familiar spirits are becoming very popular among men as men's discerners grow dim.

The New-Age group and Eastern mysticism have already permeated the rich and the famous and those that seek to be. Out-of-body experiences are actually sought after, and many are being introduced to the power of such things openly.

Satan, in his inferiority, will attract preachers and people of inferiority to present his deceiving powers to the world, building up to his master fireworks display of the false prophet and the Antichrist himself. Too bad he can't get the drift that the end is also the end for him.

Beware of preachers who build doctrines on isolated texts. Beware of those that are exceptionally attracted to demon exorcising and the spectacular. Beware of those who make excuses for their sins and blame others for them. Beware of those who draw you into deep realms of spiritual warfare and overemphasize the need to address Satan and demons all the time. Beware of those who are led by dreams and visions more than by the written Word. They may not be false, but they do need to be watched.

Be sharp to discern the difference between flesh, noise, activities, and the true Spirit at the altar calls and in meetings. Many people have trouble discerning between emotions and God. In the nineties, you will have to have very keen discernment. This is very possible, by the way.

JESUS PREDICTED AN END UNPRECEDENTED

Again, I remind you that the scriptures that follow are only a few of the many. You should do research of your own in this area. I have quoted from the Gospel of Matthew, using it as our text. There are even more scriptures as you read the other gospels.

> *"And ye shall be hated of all men for my name's sake: but he that <u>endureth to the end</u> shall be saved."*
>
> Matthew 10:22

> *"The enemy that sowed them is the devil; the harvest is the end of the world; and the reapers are the angels.*
>
> *As therefore the tares are gathered and burned in the fire; so shall it be in the end of this world.*
>
> *The Son of man shall send forth his angels, and they shall gather out of his kingdom all things that offend, and them which do iniquity;*
>
> *And shall cast them into a furnace of fire: there shall be wailing and gnashing of teeth.*
>
> *Then shall the righteous shine forth as the sun in the kingdom of their Father. Who hath ears to hear, let him hear."*
>
> Matthew 13:39-43

15

"And ye shall hear of wars and rumours of wars: see that ye be not troubled: for all these things must come to pass, but the end is not yet."

Matthew 24:6

"And this gospel of the kingdom shall be preached in all the world for a witness unto all nations; and <u>then shall the end come</u>."

Matthew 24:14

"Teaching them to observe all things whatsoever I have commanded you: and, lo, I am with you always, <u>even unto the end</u> of the world. Amen."

Matthew 28:20

16

CHAPTER 3
THE GREATEST REVIVAL

A NEW WAVE COMING

Can you feel it in the air? Can you sense it in your spirit? Do you find yourself talking about it most of the time?

I find myself meditating in it constantly and, in fact, searching it out desperately as though I'll die without it.

All over the land both ministers and laypeople are being alerted. The trumpet is being sounded. Foundations are being shaken. God is about to move in a most definite and yet unusual way.

There is a new wave of His Spirit coming to us. We will be more powerful than ever. God will use us in a very demonstrative way. Are you ready?

I believe many of the Bible prophets could see this day coming. One of those prophets, Micah, surely had spiritual insight of the day we live in. The passage of scripture in Micah 2:12-13 really defines to us what God is about to do in this next outpouring.

God's will is that we come together, very often, to worship, pray, and be fed the bread of life. It's amazing how fast we grow cool, weak, and become disoriented when we don't come together often enough.

All over the land people are crying, "Weary!" They are proclaiming how worn out they are and how much they need rest. They are wanting their pastor to cancel midweek service or Sunday evening service. But I tell you, God is not telling us to go home but rather to rally together.

Not everyone will get in this revival. In fact, only a few, a small amount, will listen to the Spirit of the Lord. In every revival we see people who get in and those who stand back and watch. I hope you'll have ears to hear what the Spirit is saying to the Church.

I tell you, friend, goats and wolves won't have much to do with this revival. The emphasis will be discipline, holiness, and authority, and there will be both a demonstration of God's Spirit and a large demand placed on each of us.

"Like sheep in a fold . . ." I believe this revival will grip the local churches. It will promote church vision, and we will feed in our good pastures. Hallelujah!

We are going to be filled to overflowing. Many will come to the house of the Lord in this hour. We will be noisy, but not the noise we've been used to. I believe we will hear shrieking and screaming as people are delivered from demons. We will hear loud cries as people get healed and touched by the Lord.

Get ready, friend, for the religious person next to you to be gone and be replaced by a hurting, needy, hungry person.

Praise God! We are going to be set free from hurt, sickness, and the oppression of our souls. We are going to be led out by our King, and we are going to be rejoicing in it.

We are going to become the greatest evangelists ever. We will feel the power of God on us to deliver people. We will become experts at discipling people in God's house.

I encourage you believers to get hooked up to this revival spirit. Don't sit around wondering what is going on or why it is going on. Don't meditate on the change, or the leadership change, or the shakiness of the hour.

Put your eyes on the Lord Jesus, and open your mind and spirit to the move of this hour. You will not be sorry!

CATCH THE WAVE

"Behold, I and the children whom the LORD hath given me are for signs and for wonders in Israel from the LORD of hosts, which dwelleth in mount Zion."

Isaiah 8:18

There is a powerful wave of God's Spirit now moving across the land. It's like a humongous cloud full of God's greatness and his best. It's a glory cloud. It's a cloud of power which will deliver, heal, charge, and challenge the people of the earth. The powers of darkness will melt and run off like a stream of debris, flowing away from believers as though driven by a mighty wind.

The remnant of God's people will be pure and awesome in power. Their behavior, itself, will put a great fear and trembling in the hearts of the wicked.

There has never been anything like it, neither will there ever be again. Some will call it a revival! This won't be wrong. A revival it will be, and yet it will be so powerful that it will be considered and remembered as more than a revival. A revival simply is people coming to sit once again at the feet of Jesus and hungering and thirsting for **him**, and Jesus obliging them.

You see, people serve the Lord to such a degree that they soon are consumed with their visions, goals, projects, programs, doctrines, and even the brethren. Without even purposing it, we soon lose track of Jesus, himself. We soon begin to quarrel, divide, and get restless. Our programs become dull and not satisfying and begin to fail.

Revival is when we stir up our hunger and thirst, go back to the Bible basics, and God meets us there. Revival is always twofold: 1) Man hungering, thirsting, and drawing nigh to God, and 2) God feeding, giving drink, and drawing nigh to man.

When man and God draw nigh to each other, it is the most powerful, most demonstrative union in all of creation. God loves man. God loves man to be godly.

> *"Arise, shine; for thy light is come, and the glory of the LORD is risen upon thee."*

Isaiah 60:1

This is it! Catch that wave! God's glory is rising upon us. We won't have to muster it up, pray it through, or borrow it from another. It will rise upon us, and it will be bright with light and quite glorious.

> *"For, behold, the darkness shall cover the earth, and gross darkness the people: but the LORD shall arise upon thee, and his glory shall be seen upon thee."*

Isaiah 60:2

20

This is one reason the remnant will be so bright and outstanding. I predict that very gross sin and behavior will consume people. The result of this wickedness will cause great diseases and the transmission of foul things, **but** God's people will be overcomers and powerful adversaries to these dark happenings.

Don't miss out on this great outpouring of God's Spirit. **Catch this wave!**

This wave will come upon us as the joy of our hearts. We've been waiting for so long to have this kind of power and this kind of glory. I'm telling you, friends, we will finally be able to do what we've talked so long about doing. We've been confessing great things, and we've been visualizing mass evangelism, and now they have come upon us. Hallelujah! Praise God!

I predict that with this glory will come great joy and rejoicing. Much noise will be made by praising saints. Many people will come out to sing and shout about God's goodness. What a marvelous and wonderful thing.

Do all you can and sacrifice all you can to be a part of it!

TWO CLOUDS APPROACH US

There is a powerful wave of God's Spirit now moving across the land. It's like a gigantic cloud full of God's greatness and his best. It's a glory cloud. It's a cloud of power which will deliver, heal, charge, and challenge the people of the earth. The powers of darkness will melt and run off like a stream of debris, flowing away from believers as though driven by a mighty wind.

God instructed me several months ago to both warn his people of the darkness, decay, and destruction that is coming, as well as reveal the things of the new revival. We've got to know both sides.

Of course, we all know that Satan will not allow this to happen without a fight. You can count on there being counterfeits and counter moves. If God is going to pour out his grace, Satan will pour out his darkness. Thank God for Romans 5:20, ". . . where sin abounded, grace did much more abound."

Listen, friend, if a wave of God's glory and God's gifts is coming upon us, then the devil will put a wave of his darkness upon the earth. God's wave will overcome and swallow up Satan's wave. God's wave will manifest on his remnant. Satan's wave will probably manifest on the rest.

> *"For, behold, the darkness shall cover the earth, and gross darkness the people . . ."*
>
> Isaiah 60:2

The cloak of darkness is now beginning to hover over the earth. It's like a deep fog. It blurs the vision and disorientates the human compass. People get lost in it, and it breeds fear. There seems to be no end to it. It is covering the whole earth. They call it AIDS, cancer, despair, gloom, etc. Only the glorious light of Christ can shine through it. I'm going to keep my light burning. How about you?

Gross darkness will cover the people. Gross to me means maximum, no room for more. This is already happening. People (even some Christian people) are snared and have been enticed by pornography, perverted sexual acts, extreme abuse of drugs, alcohol, and the like.

Suicide and murder are partners in this darkness. It was reported to me the other day that a young man from a Christian home had committed perverted sexual acts with his pet animal. Another reported that a man had raped his almost infant daughter. Listen to me! If this isn't gross darkness, I don't know what it is. I wish I could say that no Christian anywhere is caught up in any of these things, but I cannot. God will put his glory upon the **remnant**, and **they** will overcome. Are you part of it?

I believe we each have a choice to make that can change our destiny. Jesus also taught us this as he predicted the end-time conditions. I don't believe God wants anyone to live outside of grace or to be willingly disobedient. God wants each of us to be part of his remnant—those people who are hungering, thirsting, and chasing after him.

Judgment, darkness, famines, and destructions will hit planet Earth. The good news is that the remnant will be overflowing with righteousness. I look at it this way: There are two sides—darkness versus light, good versus bad, sweet versus bitter, pains of destruction versus fruits of righteousness.

Right in the midst of poverty and lack will be plenty. The unjust will have empty barns, and the just will have full barns. The remnant will be clean, not dirty; healed, not sick; sweet, not bitter; upright mouths, not gossips; good reputations, not bad reputations; and consecrated lifestyles, not permeated with the world, the flesh, and the devil.

God honors right living. God rewards diligent seekers. God answers righteous men's prayers. Chase after God, and be in the line for reward, blessing, deliverance, and his portion for you. Listen, friend, you've got to beat the devil! Fight off his trickery and walk as uprightly as you can. God will do the rest.

FRESH AIR

I was thinking the other day about the word **revival**, what it really means and all the different connotations and synonyms associated with that word. I thought about what people really need today, and I determined that probably the greatest need among people today is freshness. I'm viewing revival as fresh air today. That's right, fresh air! Fresh air is what you smell and breathe after a nice spring rain falls upon the earth—wiping some of the smog and other pollutants out of the air, washing it down upon the sidewalks, off into the curbs, and down into the gutters. The smell of freshness—to inhale and breathe cleaner air—is such a privilege and a blessing.

Fresh air is when you and your spouse, the one you love and live with, have been living tensely—maybe just a little argumentative, or not walking in perfect unity, spatting, and quarreling—and then you decide to make up. That's fresh air! It clears the air. Repentance clears the air; asking forgiveness clears the air.

Fresh air is when you and a friend, or you and a colaborer, did not see eye to eye. Your conversation became tense and your disagreement grew and you turned from friendly disagreement to debating with one another about your beliefs, or the way a certain thing should be done and doing it all in love and humility and watching it all work out fine.

Fresh air is when you are able to tell your side of the story, show your friend what you see and how you feel, and him telling you. Fresh air is knowing that your friend understands you, you understand him, and you are repairing that working relationship. All of a sudden it's a joy again to go back on duty in the house of the Lord and do your job. Repentance, forgiveness, explanation, understanding, etc., all bring fresh air. Latter rain will bring fresh air to the church in this hour.

In Acts 2:1-4 we read the account of the glorious Day of Pentecost—at least the Pentecostal season—in which the Holy Ghost fell upon those who were in the Upper Room. I know you have probably heard many sermons from this passage of scripture, but at the same time, there are some important things here for us in **this** hour.

First, let's look at the phrase "one accord." This is what we need to get into today if we're going to have fresh air and fresh outpouring. We need to get in one accord. "One accord" means "a harmonious union of sounds," not chanting and not cadence; but rather all of us saying the same thing, things like: "God, help me. God, forgive me. Lord, cleanse me. Lord, use me. Lord, I'm hungry for you." Each of us crying out to the Lord in this hour from our homes, jobs, and places of worship will invite God to do for us just what he did here in Acts, chapter two. We will feel and see and hear a sound from Heaven, a visitation from on High.

Second, let's look at the phrase "in one place." It doesn't just mean to be in one building, though in this particular passage of scripture they were. To "be in one place" means to "be equal in desire"; it means to be hooked up with the same vision. It means to be doing the same thing—not a lower place, not a higher place—but all of us coming to the same place of service. Also, "to be in one accord, in one place" means a "consent of opinions and wills." We've got to consent our opinions and our wills, so that we're all taking on

25

the opinion of the Word of God, and our wills are the will of the Father. I can't wait for some of our churches to experience a new, fresh, rushing, mighty wind—a sound from Heaven— restoring and adding the fire of the Lord Jesus to the Church today.

No, I'm not teaching that we need to go back to the Book of Acts! The Book of Acts is the Church in its embryo stage. We are to be in mature, full-grown stage. The Bible says in several places that we are to grow up, a full man, a whole body, grown up in the things of the Lord. Let's not just look back at what the early apostles had and covet. Let's look at today with today's apostles, prophets, evangelists, pastors, teachers, and believers, and let's receive what the Lord has for our churches **today**!

REVIVAL IN THREE PARTS

The Lord showed me that there would be three parts to this revival. First, He was going to visit the active Church with judgment, followed by anointing. The believers that faithfully serve Him will be supercharged and will be able to not only charge ahead themselves, but they will be able to help others also. This outpouring is not meant to just fortify the believer. Much of what God plans takes in the hurting, suffering, and lost parts of society.

The second wave of this outpouring will be for the sinners. Many people from around the world will be saved in this decade. Those who have been under the iron and bamboo curtains will have salvation like never before. Even in our own country there will be many people brought to the Lord.

26

I predict that even some of our relatives will begin to come to us and ask for spiritual help and interpretations for the times. Many from the streets and the gangs will come in. We will hear of mass salvations in different parts of the world. Some of the greatest evangelists of all times are about to be sent out. The Church is about to cast its nets into the deep for its greatest catch yet. Alleluia!

The third wave of this great, last-day revival will be for the backsliders and those who don't actively serve the Lord, though they claim to be Christians. The Lord showed me that he has a whole army out there that does not report for daily duty. They are hurt, mad, rejected, prejudiced, etc; and they do not go to church anywhere. Some of them don't even pray regularly or study the Word.

God is going to revive those who are secretly crying out to him for help. We will see many prodigals come home soon. Also, we will see many hurt and maimed people healed of their broken hearts. God is going to mend the casualties so they can walk with us once again.

DISCERNING OF SPIRITS—A PRIMARY GIFT

The Lord has shown me that the gift of discerning of spirits will be very prominent among those who walk with him. He divides severally, as He wills, you know. The Lord will equip many believers with this gift, and it will be the very thing that saves many of them from horrible crises. Many families and ministries will be protected by this manifestation of the Spirit.

Even so, the believers who will endure until the end will have to develop a discernment through the meat of the Word.

Hebrews, chapter five, teaches us that those who have matured on the Word are skillful in the word of righteousness, and they have had their senses exercised to discern from good and evil.

Baby Christians don't have a lot of discernment from good and evil. They will say, "Amen," to Jesus, and curse the devil with foul language at the same time. They will sit in church and sing, but light up a smoke as soon as they hit the door to leave. They just have a difficult time knowing the difference. After they have been Christians for awhile, and have grown in the Word, and have had their senses exercised, they will do better.

God intends for us to live by this discernment. There will be times when He will supernaturally "kick in" with the gift, though, to help us.

In the nineties believers will have a much keener discernment in the workplace and neighborhood. We will do much better at deciphering error, false ministers, and demonic presence. Don't be mistaken, this will not be an automatic thing. Many, many people will live in laziness, apathy, denial, and rebellion and, thus, suffer much.

Just a note here. Believers are going to be much more anointed than at any other time. The gifts of the Spirit will be manifest in the lives of believers. At the strangest times, God will manifest himself through his people (who are for signs and wonders anyway).

Yes, even the fruit of the Spirit will be seen in the everyday lives of the Christians. Praise God!

EVEN THE RICH

I see in the Spirit that even the rich will be actively involved in preaching the gospel. I know that many of them are now, but not like they're going to be. Many of them have stored up for years, thinking it was their talents, abilities, and hard work. Really it was God using them to collect an abundance of finances, and now he's going to call them in to help finance the gospel and the greatest harvest ever.

I also see that because of economic crises, many large companies will be forced to unload their goods. I see that they will trade their goods for a tax receipt from the church. I see computer systems, vehicles, aircraft, buildings, etc., coming to the ministry through this means. Much of it will be given and much will be purchased at extremely low prices.

I see also that most of the churches, ministries, and believers will be living debt free. The attitude of Christians towards the debt system will be one of betrayal. Most Christians will go without before they will sign for things. It will take some a long time to actually be free from debt and the credit system, but many will win the battle over it. Many wise businesspeople will come in and help the poor and uneducated to build businesses and to handle their money better.

CHAPTER 4
CHRISTIANS AND THE COURTS

"Therefore is the kingdom of heaven likened unto a certain king, which would take account of his servants.

And when he had begun to reckon, one was brought unto him, which owed him ten thousand talents.

But forasmuch as he had not to pay, his lord commanded him to be sold, and his wife, and children, and all that he had, and payment to be made.

The servant therefore fell down, and worshipped him, saying, Lord, have patience with me, and I will pay thee all.

Then the lord of that servant was moved with compassion, and loosed him, and forgave him the debt.

But the same servant went out, and found one of his fellowservants, which owed him an hundred pence: and he laid hands on him, and took him by the throat, saying, Pay me that thou owest.

And his fellowservant fell down at his feet, and besought him, saying, Have patience with me, and I will pay thee all.

And he would not: but went and cast him into prison, till he should pay the debt.

So when his fellowservants saw what was done, they were very sorry, and came and told unto their lord all that was done.

Then his lord, after that he had called him, said unto him, O thou wicked servant, I forgave thee all that debt, because thou desiredst me:

Shouldest not thou also have had compassion on thy fellowservant, even as I had pity on thee?

And his lord was wroth, and delivered him to the tormentors, till he should pay all that was due unto him."

Matthew 18:23-34

This is the attitude of many people today, including some Christians. They, themselves, have been forgiven much but won't forgive others. This unforgiveness mixed with lawless living will lead many into judgment. The Lord never has—won't now, and never will—permitted his children to behave in such ways.

One of the best ways to live in peace is to forgive everybody. To forgive someone doesn't mean all the hurt goes away. Many people wait until the hurt goes away before

31

they forgive. This is dangerous. You forgive immediately ... seven times seventy in one day.

The healing process begins once you've made the decision to forgive. Until you take the first step to forgive, you will never forget the fault or hurt. The person you hold a grudge against will live in your mind and constantly be found in your mouth.

The hurt usually takes a healing process to delete. Time and the love of Christ will help you. It almost never goes away overnight. Forgiveness is the act of your releasing another person from a violation against you. It is a quality decision that you make.

Once you have made the decision to forgive, the healing process begins.

DON'T WRESTLE WITH PEOPLE

"For we wrestle not against flesh and blood, but against principalities, against powers, against the rulers of the darkness of this world, against spiritual wickedness in high places.

Wherefore take unto you the whole armour of God, that ye may be able to withstand in the evil day, and having done all, to stand."

Ephesians 6:12-13

Learn **now** that it is not permissible to live an argumentative life. It is a violation of the Holy Scriptures for you and me to be in strife with others. If you entertain strife, you will begin to invite every evil work (see James 3:14-17). The last thing you need in your marriage is every evil work. The last thing you need in your body is every evil work. The last thing you need in your family is every evil work. The last thing you need in your ministry is every evil work.

I can promise you, if you live a life of quarrelling, holding grudges, and blaming others, it will lead you away from your life's call and place you back in the flesh. You will end up troubled and crippled spiritually. This is not the will of God for you.

Nobody or nothing should be so important to you that you would allow them or it to take you off course or to hurt you spiritually.

You will always find people in churches who want their own way, and they will go to every extreme to get it. They talk all the right charismatic talk and perform most of the actions, but at the same time hurt, maim, and destroy. These people will contend with you. They will pick a fight with you. Learn **now** how to respond to these fleshly challenges.

RAMPAGING IS RAMPANT

Wake up to the facts, folks. There are many people who have no ethics at all and no comprehension of damages done by their violations. You be careful that you are not caught up in it.

I've watched some so-called Bible college graduates come to certain cities and rip and tear at what is there. They will build their work at anybody else's expense. It doesn't seem to matter much to them that they are not really helping the Kingdom. Their own self-promotion and advancement seems to be preeminent. Watch out for these people. They will use anything and anybody to promote their cause and projects.

CHRISTIANS SUING CHRISTIANS

Like never before, Christian people are taking Christian people to the civil courts to settle disagreements. You will see even more of this as the Day approaches. This is, of course, contrary to the way of Christ. Man's way says, "Pay them back; make them pay; stone them." Calvary says, "Forgive them, they know not what they do."

There needs to be a revival of humility in the hearts of Christian people. Whatever happened to, "Let the righteous smite me, and I will consider it an anointing oil" and "Those who love the law of God—nothing by any means shall offend them"? What about, "Judge not lest ye be judged"?

I know that there are true violations, and many times these cause deep hurts; but even still, we must find ways of dealing with them without turning to the world as mediator.

Jesus never did, and doesn't now, expect us to turn away from Bible ways and turn to the world's principles. I include divorce in this. I know that divorce is a very perplexed issue, and very painful for all involved, but it still seems to me that two people who love Jesus could settle much of this without worldly intervention.

Not only are Christians suing each other, but other people are dragging the church to court. We have everything from tax violations to malpractice suits. The more Christians enter the world to deal with or stand against the issues of the day, the more the world will strike back. We are not going to stop either thing. Prepare yourself for that day.

Get your books in order and deal with things properly. I mean this for your home as well as your ministry. We must do things uprightly at all times. If you don't know what to do or how to do it, then seek out both professional help as well as spiritual.

> *"When thou goest with thine adversary to the magistrate, as thou art in the way, give diligence that thou mayest be delivered from him; lest he hale thee to the judge, and the judge deliver thee to the officer, and the officer cast thee into prison.*
>
> *I tell thee, thou shalt not depart thence, till thou hast paid the very last mite."*
>
> Luke 12:58-59

> *"And when they bring you unto the synagogues, and unto magistrates, and powers, take ye no thought how or what thing ye shall answer, or what ye shall say:*
>
> *For the Holy Ghost shall teach you in the same hour what ye ought to say."*
>
> Luke 12:11-12

CHAPTER 5
HEIGHT OF PERVERSIONS

"Were they ashamed when they had committed abomination? nay, they were not at all ashamed, neither could they blush . . ."

Jeremiah 6:15

"But evil men and seducers shall wax worse and worse, deceiving, and being deceived.

But continue thou in the things which thou hast learned and hast been assured of, knowing of whom thou hast learned them."

2 Timothy 3:13-14

"And as it was in the days of Noe, so shall it be also in the days of the Son of man.

They did eat, they drank, they married wives, they were given in marriage, until the day that Noe entered into the ark, and the flood came, and destroyed them all.

Likewise also as it was in the days of Lot; they did eat, they drank, they bought, they sold, they planted, they builded;

But the same day that Lot went out of Sodom it rained fire and brimstone from heaven, and destroyed them all.

Even thus shall it be in the day when the Son of man is revealed."

Luke 17:26-30

Prepare yourself **now** for the coming distractions and perversions. Even as I write this book, crime, perversion, and violence are at an all-time high. I know this shouldn't include the Church, but it does. I wish we could say that all church-goers were the example of clean-living people and all the non-churchgoers were the bad guys. However, not all bad guys are unchurched.

Much of the damage being done to the Kingdom of God is being done by its inhabitants. Why? Because people are mostly mental-assenting or emotionally connecting them-selves to Christ. Many have become dull of hearing or seared in conscience.

SEXUAL PERVERSIONS AND PORNOGRAPHY

Sexual offenses in the church have escalated, and the church has mostly failed at dealing with this dilemma prop-erly. We seem to have a mass outbreak of adultery and fornication. Maybe it's just being publicized more. Either way, it is still there, and it's like a plague. It not only grabs hold of preachers but a multitude of believers as well.

It amazes me that we have such a permissiveness and tolerance towards sensuality and pornography. I don't mean just the world, but rather the infiltration into the church. Many

Christians are entertained by "R" rated (and worse) movies and rented videos. It's a shock to the pure and an abomination to the Lord.

Even homosexuality has come totally into the public, and they who practice this sin are fighting for their rights. This sin is affecting every realm of life and has permeated into every age group. The Bible calls it an abomination to the Lord, but men (including many Christians) have made room for it. It is almost scary to think that many so-called Christian people may practice homosexuality.

> *"For this cause God gave them up unto vile affections: for even their women did change the natural use into that which is against nature:*
>
> *And likewise also the men, leaving the natural use of the woman, burned in their lust one toward another; men with men working that which is unseemly, and receiving in themselves that recompense of their error which was meet.*
>
> *And even as they did not like to retain God in their knowledge, God gave them over to a reprobate mind, to do those things which are not convenient."*
>
> Romans 1:26-28

> *"Know ye not that the unrighteous shall not inherit the kingdom of God? Be not deceived: neither fornicators, nor idolaters, nor adulterers, nor effeminate, nor abusers of themselves with mankind."*
>
> 1 Corinthians 6:9

"Without natural affection . . .

But they shall proceed no further: for their folly shall be manifest unto all men, as theirs also was."

2 Timothy 3:3, 9

Pornography has become blatant. It is seen in some American stores at the children's eye level. It is possible to obtain child porn almost without shame. Our children view things on prime-time television that were banned even five years ago. They can almost freely dial telephone porn talkers to experience perverted, sensual communications.

"Ye have heard that it was said by them of old time, Thou shalt not commit adultery:

But I say unto you, That whosoever looketh on a woman to lust after her hath committed adultery with her already in his heart."

Matthew 5:27-28

"But that we write unto them, that they abstain from . . . fornication . . ."

Acts 15:20

"It is reported commonly that there is fornication among you, and such fornication as is not so much as named among the Gentiles, that one should have his father's wife. [Incest]

And ye are puffed up, and have not rather mourned, that he that hath done this deed might be taken away from among you.

39

For I verily, as absent in body, but present in spirit, have judged already, as though I were present, concerning him that hath so done this deed,

In the name of our Lord Jesus Christ, when ye are gathered together, and my spirit, with the power of our Lord Jesus Christ,

To deliver such an one unto Satan for the destruction of the flesh, that the spirit may be saved in the day of the Lord Jesus.

I wrote unto you in an epistle not to company with fornicators:

Yet not altogether with the fornicators of this world, or with the covetous, or extortioners, or with idolaters; for then must ye needs go out of the world.

But now I have written unto you not to keep company, if any man that is called a brother be a fornicator . . ."

1 Corinthians 5:1-5, 9-11

"Know ye not that the unrighteous shall not inherit the kingdom of God? Be not deceived: neither fornicators, nor idolaters, nor adulterers, nor effeminate, nor abusers of themselves with mankind.

Flee fornication. Every sin that a man doeth is without the body; but he that committeth fornication sinneth against his own body."

1 Corinthians 6:9, 18

40

"And lest, when I come again, my God will humble me among you, and that I shall bewail many which have sinned already, and have not repented of the uncleanness and fornication and lasciviousness which they have commited."

2 Corinthians 12:21

"Marriage is honourable in all, and the bed undefiled: but whoremongers and adulterers God will judge."

Hebrews 13:4

"Ye adulterers and adulteresses, know ye not that the friendship of the world is enmity with God? whosoever therefore will be a friend of the world is the enemy of God."

James 4:4

"Even as Sodom and Gomorrha, and the cities about them in like manner, giving themselves over to fornication, and going after strange flesh, are set forth for an example, suffering the vengeance of eternal fire.

Likewise also these filthy dreamers defile the flesh, despise dominion, and speak evil of dignities."

Jude 1:7-8

It is difficult, friend, to live clean and stay out of sin when you permit such information to enter your life. Pornography will ruin your life, family, and marriage. Satan will use it to pervert you and lead you away. God forbid that we would ever know how many Christian men hide porn magazines under their mattresses or truck seats.

VIOLATING VIRGINS

The teasing and jeering at teenage virgins has always been a problem in our school systems, but who would have guessed that it would enter the church? It is easy to see it in the midst of youth groups—even in our most reputable churches. It is still a macho achievement to steal a virgin's crown.

Condoms are definitely not the solution for teenage sex. I doubt very seriously that they will stop the plague of AIDS. Sin is the problem, and it takes the blood of Jesus to cleanse and deliver. If our children were being taught morals, they could protect themselves better.

It is very difficult to lead children away from the lifestyle of sin, when it was their own parents who violated them. In some cases, even fathers have been the ones to triumph over their daughter's virginity. How men could attend church regularly and still practice such things is beyond me, but they do. God forbid if this is becoming normal behavior or is accepted without repercussions.

If you are in any of these sins, or have been victimized by those who are, run to your pastors or parents for help. You should not be ashamed to get help. Thank God that Jesus hates only the sin and not those who are committing it. There is hope for you no matter who you are and no matter what you've done.

BEASTIALITY

Believe it or not, beastiality has begun to penetrate even some Christian people's lives. I know this is shocking, but it is a reality we can't hide from. I have had pastors tell me of situations like this that they have already dealt with or are now dealing with. The Bible forbids us to have any kind of sexual activity with any kind of animal. Don't be fooled. Protect your kids. Even some television shows and movies hint such activities between woman, man, and beast.

"Whosoever lieth with a beast shall surely be put to death."

Exodus 22:19

"Neither shalt thou lie with any beast to defile thyself therewith: neither shall any woman stand before a beast to lie down thereto: it is confusion."

Leviticus 18:23

"And if a man lie with a beast, he shall surely be put to death: and ye shall slay the beast.

And if a woman approach unto any beast, and lie down thereto, thou shalt kill the woman, and the beast: they shall surely be put to death; their blood shall be upon them."

Leviticus 20:15-16

"Cursed be he that lieth with any manner of beast. And all the people shall say, Amen."

Deuteronomy 27:21

43

I realize that some of the scripture references above are from the Old Testament, and we do not live under the curse that is affixed to that law. In the Church, it is not required of us to put anyone to death for their sins. We can rely on His grace to forgive us and cleanse us. Even so, we must understand that God is definitely not in favor of any of these practices.

I encourage you to alert yourself and protect yourself and your family from these great dangers. Every era has its perils, and every generation has its own warfare. Alert yourself to the times and defend yourself against these things. You are destined to win, if you don't give in.

> *"Were they ashamed when they had committed abomination? nay, they were not at all ashamed, neither could they blush: therefore they shall fall among them that fall: at the time that I visit them they shall be cast down, saith the LORD."*
>
> Jeremiah 6:15

CHAPTER 6
SATAN PERMEATING THE HOME

"But strong meat belongeth to them that are of full age, even those who by reason of use have their senses exercised to <u>discern both good and evil</u>."

Hebrews 5:14

"I will behave myself wisely in a perfect way. O when wilt thou come unto me? I will walk within my house with a perfect heart.

I will set no wicked thing before mine eyes: I hate the work of them that turn aside; it shall not cleave to me."

Psalm 101:2-3

One day while I was preaching, the Lord spoke to me about the homes of the families that I pastor. He took me up in the Spirit and let me look into many of these family settings. I not only saw how they were living but also heard much of what was being said in private.

As I beheld this awesome revelation, the Lord also showed me how the enemy was getting into our homes. God cares about our homes and our private lives. Satan wants in this sphere of life because he can do grave damage there.

45

Like the scripture I quoted above, I will put no wicked thing before my eyes. Even at home, I will walk in the way of righteousness. Contrary to what some say, this is possible.

Satan is permeating our homes through the airwaves and the lines of communication. He is riding these waves like a mighty warrior on a powerful stallion. Without a fight, he enters our living rooms and—in some homes—the very rooms our children sleep in.

Through the telephone lines, he rides in on the beast of gossip and talebearing. Through the television and video machines, he rides in on the beast of pornography and worldly philosophies. On the radio waves, he rides in on the beast of radical, rock-beat, sensual communications. He even comes riding into the privacy of our homes through printed matter.

I am not magnifying his work here, but rather I'm bringing your attention to a deadly enemy who is penetrating the secured perimeter of your private lives. Stop him now while you are still in control.

Deal with your children about their outrages of anger, fear, and tempers. No matter what their age is, you can help them live free. Do not permit your children to freely throw tantrums. Do not permit them to live in strife among themselves. It is more dangerous than what most parents want to admit.

There is no age limit on perversion. Once a little boy asked his pastor how old one has to be in order to watch the rest of the movie. His parents would make him leave the room whenever a "bad part" would come on the screen. They did not realize that they were breeding in their child the idea that one can enjoy or partake of perversions when you reach a certain age. This young man will grow up waiting for the day of his maturation—this is wrong!

Perversion is perversion, and lust is lust. Even people over eighteen should not partake of these kinds of things—not even in secret.

For most of you, it would be silly to get rid of your electronics. It isn't your equipment that is the problem. If you are permitting these things in your life, then you need to deal with **you**.

We all know that God is also using telecommunications to reach the unreached and tell the untold. You also can benefit spiritually from audio, video, and the printed page. Just use discretion and discipline to monitor your intake.

Be very cautious about who your children play with and as teenagers who they bring home. Many times it isn't your child at all who is bad, but rather he or she has been tainted or seduced by a worldly friend. Be strong to blockade this infiltration of satanic and worldly influence in your home.

CHAPTER 7
SATAN RECEIVING ATTENTION

"And in all things that I have said unto you be circumspect: and make no mention of the name of other gods, neither let it be heard out of thy mouth."

Exodus 23:13

Most recently I have been telling Christians everywhere to read Galatians, chapter five, to learn the difference between flesh and demons. I know that Satan is pleased with all the attention he is getting that he doesn't even earn.

It's bad enough that we Christians even have fleshly practices in our private lives, but somehow it seems magnified when we blame the devil for it. I believe we need to stop our mouths in this area.

HIGH PRAISES OF GOD ON OUR LIPS

We are to have the high praises of God on our lips and a two-edged sword in our hands. It is God that we should be praising. It is God's works in our midst that should get all the attention. Testify of what Jesus has done and is doing in your life. Learn to be silent about your problems and your attacks. Speak to your mountains and not about them.

48

When you speak and when you pray, mention the solution— not the problem. Learn **now** to pray and speak the Word of God. To open your mouth and say anything else is in direct conflict with God's supply system.

I'll remind you here that angels hearken unto the voice of the Word of God. I suppose demons hearken unto the words that magnify their master. The last thing you need is to invite demonic activity, in addition to the warfare you already face.

INTERCESSORS IN VIOLATION

Many intercessors are in violation also. They are gossiping to God. They have exalted themselves to a place that scripture doesn't give them. Many of them slyly rule their pastors and others who are in authority.

SPEAKING TO THE DEVIL

Do not pray to the devil. Do not mix your conversations between God and the devil. Do not treat prayer like it is a conference between you, God, and the devil. There is a time to confront Satan, but it isn't while you converse with God. **Do not talk to Satan in your prayer language.** There is no evidence for this in the New Testament.

Tongues are for speaking mysteries unto God (1 Corinthians 12 and 14). You do not have to call the devil names. Read Luke 4 and learn how Jesus beat the devil. Practice it. You will come away from error, and you will begin to enjoy true, spiritual things.

OVEREMPHASIS ON DEMONOLOGY

I have noticed for a long time that there is a great over-emphasis on demons and their relationship to Christians. I have cast out real demons before, and I know what they sound like and how they manifest. Most of the demon casting being done today is only addressing the flesh.

Everything is not a demon, and we should be very careful not to claim that it is. There is a time that flesh needs discipline, and you can do all the casting you want to, but nothing will change.

Be very careful of the overemphasis of the hour. Many will be deceived in this area, and they will lead others off course. Beware of seducing spirits, as well as familiar spirits. Beware of those people who are always demon-minded.

"Now the Spirit speaketh expressly, that in the latter times some shall depart from the faith, giving heed to seducing spirits, and doctrines of devils."

1 Timothy 4:1

CHAPTER 8
A RETCHING OVER TRUTH

"Now the Spirit speaketh expressly, that in the latter times some shall depart from the faith, giving heed to seducing spirits, and doctrines of devils."

1 Timothy 4:1

"For the time will come when they will not endure sound doctrine; but after their own lusts shall they heap to themselves teachers, having itching ears; . . ."

2 Timothy 4:3

"For many shall come in my name, saying, I am Christ; and shall deceive many.

And many false prophets shall rise, and shall deceive many."

Matthew 24:5, 11

Prepare yourself **now** for a barrage of deceptive doctrines, practices, and manifestations. Only those who are living in their Bibles and searching out things will be able to thoroughly discern right from wrong in these areas.

Because so many falsehoods and heresies will try to enter the Church, many will get overly suspicious. This will cause

51

turmoil, fleshly debate, and quarreling. Worst of all, it will produce schisms and the choosing of sides. These things have already begun.

TEACHERS VERSUS HOLY GHOSTERS

Some will be labeled as teachers, and others as Holy Ghosters. Those labeled as teachers will be very leery of the others and will, in many cases, rule them out completely. It will start a whole movement against anyone who flows in the gifts of the Spirit.

They will say that anyone who has demonstrations and manifestations in their meetings should be watched because they are probably not of God. It is true that there will be the false, but we should still leave room for the genuine.

We know that the scriptures tell us of false apostles, prophets, and shepherds, but there are still true ones. Some teachers will begin to say that the apostle and prophet are not needed today. In fact, some will try to discredit them and gloat over the fact that they have run them out of their cities and bound them from churches. Beware of these things.

CARDINAL DOCTRINES ATTACKED

You will be forced to search the scriptures daily to be able to sort these things out. There is now a retching over doctrines, teachings, and practices. Many of these things are so contrary to scriptures that they are easy to recognize. Others have to be discerned.

Prepare yourself for the division that is coming to the Body, for the last-days period will have perils and deceptions common only to it. We will also see some fads and extremes which ran their course in yesteryears come around again.

Hope, for believers, will be adjusted as the Church quarrels over the validity of the catching away of the Church. Part of the church will stand against the prosperity truths and will seek to be pious through poverty. There will be a worse struggle over the healing truths found in your Bible. One of the major controversies of the day will be the overemphasis on demons and warring against Satan. Many churches will be harmed forever by these extremes.

ECUMENICALISM SUGGESTED BY ANTICHRIST SPIRIT

The spirit of Antichrist will suggest that the church resolve its differences by applying the principles of ecumenicalism. This is the plan he has for the world, and it's the same plan he has for the Church. The attitude of ecumenicalism is let's get together and be one no matter what we believe and no matter how we live. It is the same spirit that was prominent in the Babel project—building a tower to Heaven. It is filled with a sense of unity that isn't genuine, and it is saturated with permissibility and hypocrisy. Watch out for it.

It is the responsibility of every Christian to seek the person of the Lord Jesus Christ and to search out the scriptures. We must know what the Bible says about these things. Do not take any man's word for it. Find out for yourself.

OLD-FASHIONED VERSUS
THE NEW AND DIFFERENT

Stick to the basics. Don't let anybody tell you that what you believe is old-fashioned or outdated. It is not. Don't be led away by those who proclaim to have something new or different or special for the day. This attraction, to be the foremost and the front-most, is one of the largest deceptions of all times. People who want to be the leaders and the pacesetters will lean on this tactic. They will try to convince you to abandon the fathers of old and run with the new, young mavericks.

This retching over truth won't be all bad because it will cause many to get into their Bibles and finally plant these truths in their hearts. It will create an intolerance for extremes and perversions in many Christians and a persistence to obey the simple, basic, redemptive doctrines of Christ.

I pray for you. May the Lord Jesus enlighten you while you sharpen your Bible skills and make your journey towards the end.

CHAPTER 9
THE DAY AND THE HOUR

Does any man really know what the day and hour will present? Yes—emphatically yes! The Bible even explains most of the events of this day.

I know that God is now revealing to his prophets (not all who call themselves prophets) the schedule and events of the end. He is going to climax the ages, and He will reveal it to His prophets, and they will help proclaim it to the masses. This is one of the ways God prewarns and prepares his people.

LISTEN, BUT WON'T BE WARNED

It's the strangest thing. Many people listen to the preachers warning them of the time, and yet they do not take warning. It's amazing how many will listen but won't make any adjustments in their lifestyles and behavior patterns.

These are the last days, but you wouldn't know it by the way people live. Their attitude and performance are proof that we have not convinced them yet that these are truly the last of the last days.

Man's condition will wax worse—if they are now living and doing wrong. This is what the scriptures teach us. Don't pray for it, but realize it is so.

*"But evil men and seducers shall wax worse
and worse, deceiving, and being deceived."*

2 Timothy 3:13

Those who purpose to live clean will grow brighter and
brighter. They will grow from glory to glory. It will be evident
to all. It will be a pleasure to witness and very thrilling and
satisfying to be one of these.

COMPARISONS OF DAYS—BY JESUS

This day is like the day of Noah. I have written this before
and preached it many times over the years. Jesus listed five
things we should look out for as he compared our time with
Noah's time.

- People would be eating (i.e., given to appetites).
- People would be drinking (i.e., socializing).
- People would be marrying.
- People would be given in marriage.
- People did not realize the hour they lived in until the ark
  door was closed. That, my friend, is exactly the way it is
  right now.

*"But as the days of Noe were, so shall also the
coming of the Son of man be.*

*For as in the days that were before the flood
they were eating and drinking, marrying and
giving in marriage, until the day that Noe
entered into the ark,*

*And knew not until the flood came, and took
them all away; so shall also the coming of the
Son of man be."*

Matthew 24:37-39

Lot and his day were another era that Jesus compared our day to. The scriptures are clear on this, and the two eras match almost perfectly. Be alerted to it. Protect yourself and your loved ones.

"Likewise also as it was in the days of Lot; they did eat, they drank, they bought, they sold, they planted, they builded;

But the same day that Lot went out of Sodom it rained fire and brimstone from heaven, and destroyed them all.

Even thus shall it be in the day when the Son of man is revealed."

Luke 17:28-30

A THIEF IN THE NIGHT

Jesus also gave us a very severe warning and alerted us to watch and pray so that when he comes, he won't catch us like a thief in the night. Unguarded, undisciplined, uncommitted Christians may have a shaky, scary ride ahead of them. The sad part? Not one of them needs to.

"For yourselves know perfectly that the day of the Lord so cometh as a thief in the night."

1 Thessalonians 5:2

"But know this, that if the goodman of the house had known in what watch the thief would come, he would have watched, and would not have suffered his house to be broken up.

Therefore be ye also ready: for in such an hour as ye think not the Son of man cometh.

Who then is a faithful and wise servant, whom his lord hath made ruler over his household, to give them meat in due season?

Blessed is that servant, whom his lord when he cometh shall find so doing."

Matthew 24:43-46

Be sure to look out for yourself and others—that you're not misbehaving or beginning to harbor unforgiveness or improper attitudes and heart conditions. The Apostle Paul warned Timothy about the perilous times. Those times that Timothy was warned about certainly include the times in which we live.

PERILOUS TIMES EQUAL PERILOUS MEN

The root of the perils that Paul told of was the misbehavior patterns of the men of the day.

"This know also, that in the last days perilous times shall come.

For men shall be lovers of their own selves, covetous, boasters, proud, blasphemers, disobedient to parents, unthankful, unholy,

Without natural affection, trucebreakers, false accusers, incontinent, fierce, despisers of those that are good,

Traitors, heady, highminded, lovers of pleasures more than lovers of God;

Having a form of godliness, but denying the power thereof: from such turn away.

For of this sort are they which creep into houses, and lead captive silly women laden with sins, led away with divers lusts,

Ever learning, and never able to come to the knowledge of the truth."

2 Timothy 3:1-7

CHAPTER 10
SOLD OR SOLD OUT?

"No man can serve two masters: for either he will hate the one, and love the other; or else he will hold to the one, and despise the other. Ye cannot serve God and mammon."

Matthew 6:24

"In that day, he which shall be upon the housetop, and his stuff in the house, let him not come down to take it away: and he that is in the field, let him likewise not return back."

Luke 17:31

"And the cares of this world, and the deceitfulness of riches, and the lusts of other things entering in, choke the word, and it becometh unfruitful."

Mark 4:19

WHAT ABOUT YOUR STUFF?

The peril and final story of many people will be the grave accumulation of stuff. That's right, stuff. What stuff? Your stuff. What kind of stuff? The stuff you buy for yourself that has no eternal value and only weights you down. The stuff that costs you so much money. The stuff that you went in debt for. The stuff that takes most of your time to enjoy.

Jesus knew that our stuff would be a very close attachment. He taught that some people of the last day would be tempted to go into their houses to fetch their stuff—even in the last moments.

PREACHERS IN IT FOR THE MONEY

I've heard people say for years that the preachers are in it for the money. I suppose that there is a minister or two that has the wrong motive and even does wrong because of it. However, most Christian ministers are very honest, humble, and clean-living people.

It's not the minister that is in it for the money—believe me! This is a phrase that Satan has monumentalized in the minds of many people. I hear this often when people want to scrutinize the preacher. Did you ever consider that it's the minister that lets you come hear him preach and speak without cover charges or admission at the door. No tickets are sold, and you are not thrown out if you don't give in the offering.

Many people attend church services all over this nation that don't tithe or give a penny in the offerings, but the preacher lets them keep coming. I have never seen the police called on the scene when someone was mooching off the sermon or didn't pay the minister for his services.

No, no! Listen to me. Perhaps you should meditate in the truth on this matter. Have you ever gone into the grocery store, filled up your cart, and just pushed it out? You would be prosecuted (not persecuted) for shoplifting by the grocer. Yet I have never heard a person at the checkout line telling the grocer he is a crook, or a cult, or in it for the money. No, we just pay—no matter how much.

The same is true with hospitals, doctors, dentists, and the rest of the medical field. No money—no service—no insurance—little or no help; yet I have never heard anyone stand in a doctor's office or hospital and yell "cult" or "in it for the money." The list is long and the stories true. No offense to the people involved, but the system seems to work this way.

I'll remind you that it's the preacher that permits you to mooch and receive benefit without penalty if you don't pay. You'll still be invited back. Get it straight!

DECEITFULNESS OF RICHES

Jesus Christ taught us about the deceitfulness of riches. What is that? It is the idea that if I only had more, my problems would be over. This, however, is not so. That's why it is deceiving. If you abuse ten dollars, you will abuse one hundred. If you will abuse one hundred dollars, you will abuse one thousand, and so on.

The truth on riches is don't love it, don't seek it, and when you get it, don't let it rule you. Master money, and you have mastered mostly all of life. Learn to be faithful with the least, and the Lord will make you ruler over more and more valuable riches.

MAMMON OR CHRIST?

Many people say they serve Christ, but their money proves differently. If you took everything you own in your life and piled it up outside and put a value on it, and then did the same with all that you've done for the house of the Lord, you would see what I mean. The piles would not be anywhere near the same.

I've watched people over the years quibble with Master Jesus over ten percent of their money (tithe), and yet they will pay a much higher percentage to MasterCard and hardly even figure it. You can say whom you serve, but the proof is in your accounting.

Why? Jesus told us. The lust of other things entering in our hearts chokes out the Word of God that is sown there.

OVEREXTENSION IN ECONOMIC CRISES

Many ministers, churches, and Christian people overextended themselves in economic crises. They were doing good on the job, so they took on more things to pay on time. Time went by, and the good supply made a turn to lean. All of a sudden, the bills can't be paid, and the pressure is on—just like Satan knew it would be.

Many pastors have over-borrowed during plump times (in church attendance), and then when a few people left the church, or the economy changed, the offerings went down, and the torment went up. Many have literally lost their buildings and machinery.

Learn **now** to live outside of and far away from debt. Sign for nothing. If you use your charge cards, do it when you already have the money in the bank to cover them. Let God supply before the fact instead of after. Don't lean on and trust God for a few days, and then turn to your VISA card when he doesn't come through on time.

Satan is hoping that you will sell out to the lust of the flesh and the eyes. He is expecting you to do what many others have done. He has planned that you will sell yourself out to the flashy, shining goodies of this world. Fool him!

CHAPTER 11
THE CRIPPLING EFFECT
OF SELF-DECEPTION

"But be ye doers of the word, and not hearers only, deceiving your own selves.

For if any be a hearer of the word, and not a doer, he is like unto a man beholding his natural face in a glass:

For he beholdeth himself, and goeth his way, and straightway forgetteth what manner of man he was.

But whoso looketh into the perfect law of liberty, and continueth therein, he being not a forgetful hearer, but a doer of the work, this man shall be blessed in his deed."

James 1:22-25

Probably the most detrimental form of deception is self-deception. Many of the so-called exorcists of the day are busy in all kinds of spiritual warfare yet are themselves in self-deception.

As I mentioned earlier in this book, many people hear the warnings but don't take warning. They know the storm is coming but don't do anything about it.

ROCK OR SAND

Remember the story Jesus told about the two men that built their houses. One built on the sand and the other on a rock. Both of these men heard the Word, and both of them built, but one of them did what he had learned, and the other didn't. The man who did the Word was still standing strong when the flood was over. The man in self-deception was wiped out.

SHEEP OR GOAT

Jesus also taught us the story about sheep and goats. The goats were right there with the sheep until Jesus, himself, separated them. They were not permitted to enter Heaven. No one could have convinced these people that they were not true sheep. After all, they were right there with the others all the time.

The difference between the sheep and goats was not what they believed, or what they confessed, as much as what they did or didn't do. That's right, it was their performance that was judged. Goats are the epitome of self-deception.

RELENTLESS PERFORMANCE

Guard yourself against the crippling effect of self-deception. Stand against this sly, deadly practice. Make it your life's effort to practice the principles of God that you have learned—and do it relentlessly. There may be more riding on it than you think.

When you sit under your pastors and preachers and "amen" their ministries but don't practice what you've learned, then you are crippling yourself. Your mind will acknowledge the sermon, but there will be no performance that follows. This is extremely dangerous.

King Saul, who was once anointed of God through the prophet of God, was eventually doomed by his practice of self-deception. You see, he had a major problem that many people have today. He said one thing and did another. He believed one thing and practiced another.

CHAPTER 12
DECADE OF DESTINY

The Year 1991 will be a year to do the basics. We will find ourselves warring against, and overcoming, the perplexities and frustrations of life. There will be a cry in the mouths of the forerunners to return to the Bible doctrines. A much-needed stability will come to many in the body of Christ.

While many return to making the Bible preeminent in their lives, others will stray even further from the truth. Deception and deep diversions will be the peril of many. Perversion will enter the churches, and it will actually launch false ministries. These false ministries will be easily accepted by many who are hungry for spectacular things.

True ministries will enjoy the truth, as well as a divine outpouring of grace. They will rise with a new freshness and zeal that will encourage many. Look for even more corrective preaching. This is not so popular as it is lifesaving. Warnings, rebuke, reproof, and corrective preaching will rescue many— as brands plucked out of the burning fire.

The word for this coming year will be **proliferate.** God woke me on November 14, 1990, about 3:00 a.m. to tell me this. Ten times, very loudly, the Lord spoke to me that the ministry and Church would be **prolific** in their march towards the end.

The word **proliferate** means "to reproduce new parts in quick succession, to grow by multiplying, to multiply rapidly, to increase profusely." The word **prolific** means "to produce many young, or much fruit, to be fruitful and abounding." This is our word for the year. Even many small churches and ministries will increase at a rapid growth as the harvest comes upon us.

The Lord dealt with me on the requirements for good, clean living for these times. Among some of the things He said were things to get and things to get rid of. Following is a list and a short explanation of these ten things.

THINGS TO GET

GET committed to God's work. It is past the time of preparation and well into the time of performance. It is our day to show forth, stretch forth, and be committed. Talking commitment is far below having it. Talk is usually cheap unless it is backed by performance. Get committed to God's work.

GET your family affairs in order. Right now deal with your marriage covenant, your children, your finances, your business dealings, your household things, and your relatives. Draw the line on some of the things you've left unclear and put your foot down on the things you've permitted. It is your responsibility and you must do it now. Get your family affairs in order.

GET scriptural stability in your life. Too many church-goers are scripturally unstable. They have ideas, dreams, aspirations, and such, but they are not according to Scripture. People that are wishy-washy better get lined up with the Book.

It is a very bad time to be loose. The things done that are not according to the Book are going to all burn up anyway. Get scriptural stability in your life.

GET fortification in your church life. Stop running all around from church to church like a tramp. Stop and root yourself somewhere. Once you have grounded yourself in a ministry, then perform there according to the Scriptures. Find your place in the body and start producing fruit before it's too late. Be faithful, prompt, and enthusiastic about your work. Prove yourself to God and to others. Get fortification in your church life.

GET ready for new people. Many people are going to enter the church in these last hours. They are not going to be like us. They aren't going to talk, walk, or live like we do. Of course we will help them change their lives and become more Christian, but when they first come in, they will be different. Make room for them in your head and in your congregational settings. They will need you, and you don't want to run them out. Get ready for new people.

THINGS TO GET RID OF

GET RID OF debt . . . stop spending. The first way to get rid of debt is to stop spending. At least then the money you do have will pay bills. Sure you have to tithe, sow, and direct your confession. Many people are in debt simply because they spend too much. Others are in debt because they talk too much, and the wrong way. Fast and pray and find out what your problem is and fix it, but do it now. Get rid of debt.

GET RID OF bad attitudes. As with your attitude, so goes your life. If your attitude is off, then your perspective will be off. Not only that, but you will steal your own joy and misguide your own path. You must deal with your attitude and purpose to do it daily if you plan to live right in Christ. Get rid of bad attitudes.

GET RID OF bad confessions. I could talk to you all day on this very subject. There are many scriptures on this to help you. Get a friend to help you watch your words. It's not as hard as you think it is. It mostly takes awareness and some discipline, and you will be on your way. Study the scriptures on this subject, and they will renew your mind and fix your mouth. Get rid of bad confessions.

GET RID OF unholy, unscriptural friends. That's right. The Bible warns us about those who subvert whole households with their mouths. It says they must be stopped. Also the Bible says that bad company corrupts good morals. It also informs us that a righteous person chooses his friends with discretion. No one can force you, but I strongly warn you to do it. Who you spend most of your time with is who you will be most like. Get rid of unholy, unscriptural friends.

GET RID OF fleshly, sinful practices. You can humble yourself. You can purge yourself. You can discipline yourself. The bottom line is, what you want the most is what you are going to have. Miracles don't necessarily happen where great needs are. If they did, there would be no more needs. Miracles happen most where there is a very deep want. Carnal practices that you allow in your life may be the very things that are your worst enemy. They could be costing you the greatest price. Get rid of fleshly, sinful practices.

> *"Because thou servedst not the LORD thy God with joyfulness, and with gladness of heart, for the abundance of all things;*
>
> *Therefore shalt thou serve thine enemies . . ."*
>
> Deuteronomy 28:47-48

CHAPTER 13
REAL SHEPHERDS

I have shared this many times, but it still is worthy of sharing again. The Lord showed me that the highest commodity [the scarest and therefore most valuable] on the face of the earth would be a righteous shepherd. This is becoming more and more evident. It's a shame, but nonetheless true.

True shepherds don't run or back down from the wolves. Quite the contrary. They fortify their guard and fight for the lives of the sheep. Hirelings don't really care about the future of the sheep, but rather their own reputations and ministries.

True shepherds don't withhold truth. They speak the truth in love. They are not half as concerned for your feelings as they are for your eternal security. False shepherds and hirelings will always sweet-talk you and politic you. They will withhold the truth in trade for your favor.

True love will not fail you. It will yell out warnings that will save your life—at the cost of your hurt feelings. Hurt feelings are nothing but a violation of personal pride. Feelings are part of the flesh anyway. They mend easily and are of much less value than your eternal destiny.

SPIRIT OF CONTROL

Don't you listen to this lie! For years I have heard people shout this statement at every pastor who will discipline the flock. Basically, people don't want to be disciplined, and therefore, they resist those who do it. In most cases, it is not a spirit of control at all.

A spirit of control literally controls people and puts them under bondage. This is quite different than a leader who disciplines and leads with authority. Not all authority is bad, you know. I will be glad when the body of Christ finally learns the difference between discipline and bondage.

SHEPHERDING ERROR

Don't make the mistake that many who resist strong leadership do, protesting that they are being led into error. There is such a thing as shepherding error; but not all strong, authoritative leadership is wrong.

Some Christians are so rebellious and independent that they claim error whenever they are corrected. These same maverick-type believers will soon find themselves in perils that are too severe for them to get out of.

Sure some leaders go too far. Everybody knows this, but it is only a very small group. Most of God's leaders are not in this extreme, and they are only trying to do their job to equip you, mature you, and make you ready for ministry.

A good shepherd corrects, rebukes, reproves, and brings instruction in righteousness. Be a good little lamb and don't play shepherd. Don't pretend to be so mature. Read Ephesians, chapter four. Submit to the Bible.

NO SHEPHERD'S HEART

Most people have been raised in religion and, therefore, they have years of training that are not necessarily Bible-based. Many people have a totally wrong view of what a shepherd is. They only know what they have been taught, and many of them have been taught wrong. They only know what they have watched, and most of them have watched hirelings or religious clergy.

With this in mind, you can see why so many people misunderstand the authoritative, aggressive preachers of the day. Just because a man has a strong voice doesn't mean he has a hard heart. This is a ridiculous suggestion.

Many people say, "He doesn't have a shepherd's heart." These same folks don't even know what a shepherd's heart is. They only mean to say that they disagree with the sternness of the preacher. The body is so frail that they cannot tolerate anyone who doesn't cuddle up to them.

Many of the preachers of the day are aggressive, and they are very bold. To a frail, timid, carnal Christian, this kind of man is a threat and will be rejected as too hard or too cocky. The truth is, he is too true, and speaks too much truth, too truthfully.

LOOSENESS OR LIBERTY

Liberty does not mean looseness. Liberty means you have been freed from the slavery of sin and its fetters. It doesn't mean you don't have to submit or that you can do your own thing.

Freedom is deliverance from the driving forces of Satan and his wicked addictions. It doesn't mean you are free from discipline or from the governments of the church. Jesus set gifts in the church to help you, not to give you something to be delivered from.

Every church has rules and guidelines of how that ministry will operate in order to give you accurate, genuine help. This is not wrong. This is good. This is not what you should be seeking to be freed from.

Many people mistake the restrictions and responsibilities of Christianity as bondage and, therefore, when they backslide, they say they are free from the bondage. Actually, they have entered back into the bondage again by rejecting the restraints of the Lord. The Lord will not let you live any way you want to.

Looseness is when you cast off constraint and responsibility, and fool yourself into thinking that you can do your own thing now and no one can do anything about it. This is your flesh rejoicing that it doesn't have to be disciplined anymore. It is your flesh that is feeling so good, not your spirit.

FALSE AND TRUE SHEPHERDS

There are more false shepherds than there are false prophets or teachers. There are more shepherds than there are other fivefold ministry gifts. This is probably why the difference.

False may not always mean satanic. False doesn't always mean evil or wicked. False could just mean that they are not

75

in their right office. I don't believe it always means this, but sometimes it does.

Many ministers are trying to function in the wrong office and without a gift. This would make them false. A man without a gift and appointment from Heaven to pastor a church is a false shepherd in the eyes of the Lord Jesus. He may not be a false person or false Christian, but he is a false pastor.

So is it with false prophets, teachers, and apostles. There will be a tremendous influx of these kinds of ministers as the end comes upon us. Be on the alert for them. Watch for many of these ministers who will change positions and offices so easily.

Why would anyone pretend to be in an office or ministry that Jesus never appointed them to? Competition, jealousy, flesh, striving, confusion, seeking their own, pride, comparison, misconception, seduction, deception, familiar spirits, false prophesies—are a few reasons we can name.

There is a severely false minister and that is the one that is actually a representative of Satan, and he knows it. He has planted himself in the church to disillusion it and lead it off course. This kind of false minister will try to kill off the other ministries that are true.

True ministers thrive on the Word of the Lord, and they obey Heaven—no matter what. They are not moved by people or people's demands, and they live what they preach. Read my book *Preachers of Righteousness* to learn more on this subject.

Get ready for these true shepherds to come on the scene. Of course, many of them are here already. It isn't that they are all going to be new ministers or young ministers, it's just that they are going to be recognized like never before.

These truth-bearers are going to set a lot of things straight. They will speak unadulterated truth. They will be aggressive, bold, and courageous. They will think nothing of challenging sin and purging the church. A wonderful cleanliness will come to our churches because these men will live clean, and they will not permit open rebellion and sin.

Heaven will support these powerful preachers, and they will bring Heaven's supply with them. Healing, manifestations of the true gifts, and a demonstration of God's power will be evident. It is a glorious strength to replace the compromising and cheating of times past.

CHAPTER 14
CLIMAXING THE AGES

The Holy Spirit knows exactly what is going on today. He is God, and God knows all things. You and I don't know everything, but we know Him who knows all things. The Bible tells us that the Holy Spirit will show us things to come.

> *"Howbeit when he, the Spirit of truth, is come, he will guide you into all truth: for he shall not speak of himself; but whatsoever he shall hear, that shall he speak: <u>and he will shew you things to come.</u>"*
>
> John 16:13

I am not at all afraid of the coming days. We will be fine if we walk with God and obey him. The Bible is very clear on the times and what to expect, as well as how we are to respond.

The devil doesn't win, the church does. Sinners don't prevail, believers do. Sickness doesn't reign, healing does. Bondage doesn't rule, liberty does. Darkness doesn't triumph, the light does. It's a wonderful story with a tremendous end for the overcomer.

Overcoming is the word of the day. Not just surviving, but overcoming. Not just coping with, but overpowering. We have this treasure in earthen vessels, and we are the temple of the living God. We win. That's that!

WALKING IN THE SPIRIT

It is a must that we walk in the Spirit. He will guide us into all truths and show us things to come. He will also bring all things to our remembrance and remind us of all Jesus taught. This is proven in the Holy Scriptures.

It is not permitted for believers to walk in the flesh. Besides, if you do, you'll just be miserable and powerless. We are to break the power of sin over our lives with the name of Jesus and the blood of the Lamb.

Lust, flesh, pornography, sensuality, carnality, and the spirit of the world are not our portion, and we should resist these things with everything that is within us. Flee fornication, flee idolatry, and purge yourself daily. You can live clean even if everyone around you isn't.

It is a must for end-time believers to walk in the Spirit and to be so accurately led by him. This is no time to be off the beaten path or sidelined somewhere. The leadership of God is sure and eternal. You can trust it.

Pray and fast and work out your relationship with Him, so that you know exactly how He will deal with you. Develop your hearing inner ear so that it is keen to His nudging.

Be swift to repent and fix anything and everything that you have damaged in any way. Don't let even a day go by without turning from your faults and sins. Lay aside everything that slows you down and that brings you back into the flesh. Your sins and your weights will keep you carnal and condemned.

PRAYER EQUALS A FAMOUS WEAPON

From Genesis to Revelation we see that men and women of God overcame and overpowered their enemies through the power of prayer. Many believers today are in the sin of prayerlessness. Many have gone to such extremes in prayer that they are putting on more of a show than actually being effective. Accuracy is rapidly being replaced by zealous activities and extravaganza.

Even so, prayer is still one of your very best weapons, especially as you pray with your devotional tongues given to you through the Holy Spirit. We don't speak to the devil with this tongue, but rather we speak mysteries unto God. Our understanding is unfruitful, and we speak directly to our Father in Heaven.

Spend time in prayer getting direction for your life and ministry. Learn to listen while you are with the Lord. Practice His presence and enjoy it. Expect Him to manifest to you and be your closest friend. It is His will for you.

You will have to sort some things out, only in prayer, because they will look so genuine that only God could show you the difference. Some of these things are so dangerous that those who don't pray often will be eliminated.

THE WORD OF GOD IS OUR SWORD

The Bible teaches us that the Word is our sword. When it is spoken, it is even that much more powerful. The devil is counting on the fact that you will not read and study your Bible every day. He is working hard at keeping you away from its content. If you never pick up the Bible and practice using it, then you will never get it in your mouth. Until it gets in your mouth, its full power will never be released.

Jesus used the sword of the Spirit every time he defeated the devil in the wilderness while being tempted. He won by pointing His adversary to the recorded truths and mandates of His Heavenly Father.

Read your Bible, study it systematically, line upon line, precept upon precept, here a little, there a little, memorizing it, and meditating in it, until you are a workman that needs not to be ashamed.

It is established forever in Heaven, and God has exalted it even above his name. His name is as good as His Word. We have the divine privilege of using both. Praise God!

CHURCH ATTENDANCE
EQUALS DRAWING STRENGTH

You live in a day when you cannot afford to miss even one church service. The decay and moth-eating detriment of the world is eating up many Christians. This is no day to pretend that you can make it on your own. You cannot. We need each other like never before.

Hang around and run around with people who are motivators and not grumblers. Stay away from people who are chronic pessimists, for they will steal your courage with you hardly noticing it.

There is a power in true fellowship. True fellowship is not playing together or socializing, but working together in God.

Working together in God is what causes us to be fulfilled and satisfied. It builds us up and gives us a special sense of belonging that you can't get any other way.

Go to church and don't miss a service. The very one you miss could be the one you've waited for all your life. Besides, if the devil can figure out what keeps you out of church, he will haunt you with it.

CELEBRATION OF PRAISE AND WORSHIP

The Lord is looking for those who are true worshipers and exuberant praisers. I don't know so much about all the militant songs of the day, but I do know that if we will sing the Word of God, it will have power within itself. Learn to concentrate on Jesus as you sing these songs, so that it is him that is getting the attention.

Be worshipers at home as well. I don't mean to have a song service at home with the family. You could if you wanted to, but I mean while you are in your prayer time. Learn to sing and whistle the songs of God as you do your daily routine. Fill your heart with true thanksgiving and gratitude and watch how it changes your life.

Remember the ten lepers that Jesus cleansed? One of them came back and fell at His feet and worshiped Him with thanksgiving. Jesus made him totally whole. There is a great difference between being cleansed and made whole. I'm for being made whole.

When you do go to church or listen to music tapes, enter in. Refuse to pervert the music of the kingdom by using it for entertainment in any way. In church, always enter into worship. Do as the songleader does until you learn it and can do it spontaneously. You will never again be the same.

COMMUNION EQUALS FELLOWSHIP WITH GOD

In these awesome last days, it is easy to take on carnal traits and pick up the philosophy of the world. We get so busy, we neglect not only the gift of God in us, but the very God who gave it as well. It is a must for last-day believers to know Jesus of Nazareth personally.

The Lord's table is a beautiful place to make things right as well as reminisce about the work of Calvary. It is a very good place to give thanks for the provisions of Christ and to worship him for what he has done and who he is.

Communion elements will be used to actually confront you, once again, that Jesus died for you; and church has never been a game to him.

Many are sick, many are weak, and many die early because they don't come around the Lord's table to keep things in proper perspective. We must discern the Lord's Body, both the one at Calvary, and members of his Body today.

CONCLUSION

I have written this book to alert you to some of the things that we will face in these next few years. I also wanted to bring to your attention the many snares and falsehoods that Satan will try to deceive and seduce you with.

You are one of the last-day believers. You are one of those who will help usher in the coming of the Lord. What a privilege.

You can live right with God and be pleasing in his sight. It is not impossible to do this. Many are already, and many more are going to. You consecrate yourself, and God will do a work of sanctification in you that will last an eternity.

If the Lord returns in the next few years, you will be ready for him, and you will appreciate my challenge. If the Lord does not come, you will be fit for the years that lie ahead of us. Either way, you can't go wrong by living right in Christ.

Judge yourself and fix all you can. Walk very humbly before the Lord your God, and he will assure that you are lifted up.

"He hath shewed thee, O man, what is good;
and what doth the Lord require of thee, but to

do justly, and to love mercy, and to walk
humbly with thy God?"

Micah 6:8

I pray for you, right now, and I put myself in agreement with you, according to the Holy Scriptures, that His grace is sufficient for you and that His protection is yours for these treacherous last days.

I agree with you that you will live in divine health and enjoy a long life. I agree with you that you will destroy poverty and lack over your life and that debt will also be put to death. In Jesus' name, you will have plenty to live on and enough to help preach the gospel around the world.

SINNER'S PRAYER

YOU CAN BE SAVED FROM ETERNAL DAMNA-TION and get God's help now in this life. All you have to do is humble your heart, believe in Christ's work at Calvary for you, and pray the prayer below.

"Dear Heavenly Father:

I know that I have sinned and fallen short of Your expectations of me. I have come to realize that I cannot run my own life. I do not want to continue the way I've been living, neither do I want to face an eternity of torment and damnation.

I know that the wages of sin is death, but I can be spared from this through the gift of the Lord Jesus Christ. I believe that He died for me, and I receive His provision now. I will not be ashamed of Him, and I will tell all my friends and family members that I have made this wonderful decision.

Dear Lord Jesus:

Come into my heart now and live in me and be my Savior, Master, and Lord. I will do my very best to chase after You and to learn Your ways by submitting to a pastor, reading my Bible, going to a church that preaches about **You,** and keeping sin out of my life.

I also ask You to give me the power to be healed from any sickness and disease and to deliver me from those things that have me bound.

I love You and thank You for having me, and I am eagerly looking forward to a long, beautiful relationship with You."

Other Books by Mark T. Barclay

Beware of Seducing Spirits
This is not a book on demonology. It is a book about people who are close to being in trouble with God because of demon activity or fleshly bad attitudes.

Building a Supernatural Church
A step-by-step guide to pioneering, organizing, and establishing a local church.

Charging the Year 2000
This book will alert you and bring your attention to the many snares and falsehoods with which Satan will try to deceive and seduce last-day believers.

Enduring Hardness
God has designed a program for his saints that will cause each one to be enlarged and victorious. This book will challenge your stability, steadfastness, courage, endurance, and determination and will motivate you to become a fighter.

How to Avoid Shipwreck
A book of preventive medicine, helping people stay strong and full of faith. You will be strengthened by this book.

How to Relate to Your Pastor
It is very important in these last days that God's people understand the office of pastor. As we put into practice these principles, the church will grow in numbers and also increase its vision for the world.

Improving Your Performance
Every leader everywhere needs to read this book. It will help tremendously in the organization and unity of your ministry and working force.

Preachers of Righteousness

As you read this book, you will be both edified and challenged to not only do the work of the ministry but to do it with humility, honesty, and godliness.

Sheep, Goats, Wolves

A scriptural yet practical explanation of human behavior in our local churches and how church leaders and members can deal with each other.

The Sin of Familiarity

This book is a scriptural study on the most devastating sin in the body of Christ today. The truths in this book will make you aware of this excess familiarity and reveal to you some counterattacks.

The Sin of Lawlessness

Lawlessness always challenges authority and ultimately is designed to hurt people. This book will convict those who are in lawlessness and warn those who could be future victims. It will help your life and straighten your walk with Him.

The Remnant

God has always had a people and will always have a people. Dr. Barclay speaks of the upcoming revival and how we can be part of God's remnant.

To receive Dr. Barclay's publication, *Preacher of Righteousness,* and receive a complete listing of books and audiotapes (singles and series) available, contact us at the address below.

MARK BARCLAY PUBLICATIONS
P.O. BOX 588
MIDLAND, MI 48640
(517) 835-3297